YOU MUST REMEMBER THIS

# 1958

MILESTONES, MEMORIES,
TRIVIA AND FACTS, NEWS EVENTS,
PROMINENT PERSONALITIES &
SPORTS HIGHLIGHTS OF THE YEAR

TO :

FROM :

MESSAGE :

*selected and researched
by
mary a. pradt*

WARNER **W** TREASURES™

PUBLISHED BY WARNER BOOKS

A TIME WARNER COMPANY

Warner Books, Inc.
1271 Avenue of the Americas
New York, New York 10020

Warner Treasures is a
trademark of Warner Books, Inc.

 A Time Warner Company

DESIGN:
CAROL BOKUNIEWICZ DESIGN
PRINTED IN SINGAPORE
FIRST PRINTING : MAY 1995
10 9 8 7 6 5 4 3 2 1
ISBN : 0-446-91034-1

# The U.S. launched its first earth satellite, Explorer 1, on February 1.

**THE NUCLEAR SUBMARINE NAUTILUS MADE HISTORY'S FIRST UNDERSEA PASSAGE ACROSS THE NORTH POLE.**

There were numerous other scientific and space milestones. A one-pound squirrel monkey named Gordo was launched 600 miles into space December 13 in the nosecone of a Jupiter missile, from Cape Canaveral. Rescuers were unable to recover the cone after it reentered the atmosphere at 10,000 mph and plunged into the water 1,700 miles from the launch site. Gordo presumably died inside his capsu'

**Pan American** began transatlantic flights in October with Boeing 707 service between New York and Paris. New York–Rome flights were scheduled to start soon. BOAC established the New York–London route earlier in October. PanAm's first flight to New York City took 8 hours, 40 minutes.

## IN OCTOBER, THE POPULATION OF THE U.S. REACHED 175 MILLION.

# newsreel

IT WAS A ROUGH YEAR FOR VICE PRESIDENT **RICHARD NIXON**. FIRST HE WAS PELTED WITH EGGS, FRUIT, AND STONES IN LIMA, PERU, MAY 8, AND THEN A WEEK LATER HE WAS ATTACKED BY MOBS IN CARACAS, VENEZUELA. ALTHOUGH HIT BY SHATTERED GLASS, NIXON WAS NOT SERIOUSLY HURT.

On December 13, Senator **Lyndon Baines Johnson** rejected supporters' hopes for him to run for the presidency in 1960. "I don't think anybody from the South will be nominated in my lifetime. If so, I don't think he will be elected," said LBJ.

The postcard rate rose from 2 cents to 3 cents and air-mail letters from 6 cents to 7. In other postal bad news, the postmaster general announced that customers whose dogs bit a letter carrier would be responsible for picking up their own mail.

3

In Britain, Queen Elizabeth II named four Englishwomen to baronial rank, qualifying them as the first women members of the House of Lords.

**Charles de Gaulle** became French premier after the Algerian crisis brought down the French government, the twentieth since World War II. He would become the first president of the Fifth Republic.

## The Brussels World's Fair

opened in April. Before it closed October 19, an estimated 42 million attended. Its symbol was the massive Atomium, a 360-foot-high structure with a restaurant at the top. It was the first world's fair since the 1939–40 one in New York. Its theme was the peaceful use of atomic energy.

*international*

# headlines

NIKITA KHRUSHCHEV BECAME SOVIET PREMIER, REPLACING BULGANIN.

Chairman Mao Zedong and Premier Nikita Khrushchev met in Peking to iron out ideological differences and agreed that the biggest threat to world peace was Western **"imperialistic war maniacs."**

In Cuba in September, **Fidel Castro Ruz** launched his promised offensive against the Batista government and army. Leading the insurgency, along with Fidel, were Che Guevara and brother Raul Castro.

Author **Boris Pasternak**, 68, turned down the Nobel Prize for literature, for his *Dr. Zhivago*, under pressure from Soviet authorities.

5

It was the year of the **Hula Hoop!** The founders of Wham-O, Arthur Melin and Richard Knerr, heard about Australian gym classes where kids exercised with bamboo hoops. They decided to produce a plastic version for the U.S. Melin personally demonstrated the toy at playgrounds throughout southern California. By the fall of 1958, four months after the fad took hold, 25 million had been sold, at a value of more than $30 million retail. More than twenty different manufacturers made their own hoops. Ultimately sales soared over 100 million hoops. The craze spread around the world.

**Elvis Presley** joined the army March 24, becoming U.S. 53310761. He had already starred in four movies and sold over 40 million records. Fans didn't think they would live through Elvis's two-year hitch.

# cultural
# milestones

IN PARIS IN JANUARY 1958, YVES ST. LAURENT, 22, WAS HAILED AS THE HEIR TO DIOR.

**An impressionist painting, Paul Cézanne's Boy in a Red Vest, fetched a record price at auction in London. The painting was auctioned by Sotheby's for $616,000.**

**THE REAL McCOYS**

A 1958 Zenith ad promoted its "original and exclusive Space Command **remote control television tuning**": "When you come home tired, and want to watch TV . . . it's the getting up . . . that gets you down. Now . . . tune TV from your easy chair with 'Silent Sound.' . . . Just touch a button on the unit in your hand and send through space your silent command. . . . hop back and forth between two favorites on at the same time. . . . 'De-voice' an annoying, long-winded announcer."

**THERE WERE 41,920,000 TV HOUSEHOLDS IN AMERICA. THE PERCENTAGE OF AMERICAN HOMES WITH TV WAS 83.2.**

## TOP-RATED TV SHOWS OF 1958

1. "Gunsmoke" (CBS)
2. "Wagon Train" (NBC)
3. "Have Gun Will Travel" (CBS)
4. "The Rifleman" (ABC)
5. "The Danny Thomas Show" (CBS)
6. "Maverick" (ABC)
7. "Tales of Wells Fargo" (NBC)
8. "The Real McCoys" (ABC)
9. "I've Got a Secret" (CBS)
10. "The Life and Legend of Wyatt Earp" (ABC)
11. "The Price Is Right" (NBC)
12. "The Red Skelton Show" (CBS)
13. "Zane Grey Theater" (CBS)
14. "Father Knows Best" (CBS)
15. "The Texan" (CBS)
16. "Wanted: Dead or Alive" (CBS)
17. "Peter Gunn" (NBC)
18. "Cheyenne" (ABC)
19. "Perry Mason" (CBS)
20. "The Ford Show" (NBC)

## The quiz show scandals

erupted when it turned out some contests had been "fixed," and some contestants fed information in advance. "Dotto," "21," "The $64,000 Challenge," and "The $64,000 Question" all went off the air. The latter, the show that had started the craze in the first place in 1955, had given away $2,106,800 in cash and 29 Cadillacs as consolation prizes.

**WAGON TRAIN**

Actress **Jayne Mansfield** and Hungarian-born **Miklos "Mickey" Hargitay**, Mr. Universe of 1956, were married—second nuptials for both. **Rita Hayworth**, 39, married Hollywood writer-producer **James Henry Hill**, 41. It was his first, her fifth, marriage. **Jack Webb**, of "Dragnet" fame, 38, married **Jackie Loughery**, 27, Miss America of 1952, June 24 in Van Nuys, CA (her second, his third; Julie London was a previous wife of Webb). **Ingrid Bergman**, 42, married for the third time December 21 in London. Her new husband was Swedish film and theatrical producer **Lars Schmidt**, 41. **Françoise Sagan**, 22, the French novelist, married her publisher, **Guy Schoeller**, 42, in Paris March 13 (his second). **Sammy Davis**, Jr., 32, married singer **Loray White**, 23, in Las Vegas (his first marriage, her second).

# milestones

## splitsville

**ERNEST BORGNINE, 42, WAS DIVORCED BY MRS. RHODA K. BORGNINE, 34. ROCK HUDSON, 32, WAS DIVORCED BY HIS AGENT'S EX-SECRETARY, PHYLLIS, 32. EDDIE FISHER SEPARATED FROM DEBBIE REYNOLDS AND WAS BEING SEEN WITH THE WIDOW LIZ.**

# D E A T H S

**Mary Roberts Rinehart,** prolific mystery writer, novelist, and humorist died in September at 80. Total book sales estimated at 10 million copies.

**Edward Weston**, renowned photographer, 71, died near Carmel, CA. A master craftsman of photography, he avoided using color film until 1947, but when he did, the results were as spectacular as his black-and-white masterpieces.

**Helen Twelvetrees**, a fiftyish Hollywood leading lady, died of an overdose of barbiturates.

**Johnny Stompanato**, a Hollywood hoodlum who was involved with screen star Lana Turner, was stabbed to death by Cheryl Crane, 14, daughter of Turner and ex-husband Stephen Crane. The ruling was justifiable homicide; Stompanato had threatened Turner with injury or death if she split with him, and he also terrorized the teenaged Cheryl.

**Frédéric Joliot-Curie**, French physicist, died August 14 at 58.

**Georges Roualt**, French painter, died in Paris in February at age 86.

**Tyrone Power**, the famous American actor, died in November at 44. He had just married for the third time in May.

**W. C. Handy**, legendary composer of "Memphis Blues," "St. Louis Blues," and many other compositions, died in March in New York at age 84.

# celeb births

**KEITH HARING,** hugely successful artist, was born May 4, in Kutztown, PA. His brief but meteoric career started with chalk graffiti on the streets of New York. His canvases came to be worth hundreds of thousands of dollars.

**PRINCE ALBERT ALEXANDRE LOUIS PIERRE OF MONACO** was born in March to Prince Rainier III and the former Grace Kelly. He was the Grimaldis' second child and male heir presumptive.

**PRINCE,** the rock superstar, was born Prince Rogers Nelson on June 7 in Minneapolis, MN. Most sources agree it was 1958, although for a while, he and others used a 1960 birth year.

**MADONNA,** while we're speaking of one-named legends, was born Madonna Louise Veronica Ciccone, August 15, in Bay City, MI.

**MICHAEL JACKSON,** superstar, was born August 29, in Gary, IN.

**KATE BUSH,** singer, was born July 30.

**TANYA TUCKER,** country and western singer, was born October 10.

**JAMIE LEE CURTIS,** actress, was born November 22.

**MICHELLE PFEIFFER,** actress, was born April 29.

**JIMMY SMITS,** actor, was born July 9.

**DONNY OSMOND,** singer, was born December 9.

**LORENZO LAMAS,** actor son of Arlene Dahl and Fernando Lamas, was born January 20.

**HOLLY HUNTER,** actress, was born March 20.

**STEVE GUTTENBERG,** actor, was born August 24.

**RON REAGAN,** dancer / TV personality, was born May 20.

**RANDY GARDNER,** skater, was born December 2.

**SCOTT HAMILTON,** skater, was born August 28.

**ERIC HEIDEN,** speed skater, was born June 14.

**OREL HERSHISER,** baseball player, was born September 16.

**WADE BOGGS,** baseball player, was born June 15.

**RICKEY HENDERSON,** baseball player, was born Christmas 1958.

**TOMMY HEARNS,** boxer, was born October 18.

1. **at the hop** Danny & the Juniors
2. **it's all in the game** Tommy Edwards ( a new version of Tommy's 1951 hit)
3. **the purple people eater** Sheb Wooley
4. **all i have to do is dream** Everly Brothers
5. **tequila** The Champs
6. **don't** Elvis Presley
7. **nel blu dipinto di blu (volare)** Domenico Modugno
8. **sugartime** McGuire Sisters

# hit music

Other acts with top-charted singles included the Kingston Trio ("Tom Dooley"), Chuck Berry ("Sweet Little Sixteen"), the Four Preps, the Chordettes ("Lollipop"), the Royal Teens ("Short Shorts"), and Bobby Darin ("Splish Splash"). There were numerous novelty tunes besides #3, #10, and #11 at right. The Playmates did a record called "Beep Beep" in which a little Nash Rambler left its higher-octane competition in the dust.

9. **he's got the whole world (in his hands)** Laurie London
10. **the chipmunk song** The Chipmunks
11. **the witch doctor** David Seville
12. **to know him, is to love him** Teddy Bears
13. **poor little fool** Ricky Nelson
14. **it's only make believe** Conway Twitty
15. **get a job** Silhouettes

13

1. **doctor zhivago**
   boris pasternak

2. **anatomy of a murder**
   robert traver

3. **lolita**
   vladimir nabokov

4. **around the world with auntie mame**
   patrick dennis

5. **from the terrace**
   john o'hara

6. **eloise at christmastime**
   kay thompson

7. **ice palace**
   edna ferber

8. **the winthrop woman**
   anya seton

9. **the enemy camp**
   jerome weidman

10. **victorine**
    frances parkinson keyes

**bestselling**

**nonfiction**

**books**

1. **kids say the darndest things!**
   art linkletter

2. **'twixt twelve and twenty**
   pat boone

3. **only in america**
   harry golden

4. **masters of deceit**
   j. edgar hoover

5. **please don't eat the daisies**
   jean kerr

6. **better homes and gardens salad book**

7. **the new testament in modern english**
   translated by j. p. phillips

8. **aku-aku**
   thor heyerdahl

9. **dear abby**
   abigail van buren

10. **inside russia today**
    john gunther

Both college and pro basketball were growing in popularity. St. Louis, with Bob Pettit its star player, defeated Boston in NBA finals. Boston's Celtics featured the legendary Bill Russell. In NCAA action, underdog Manhattan College defeated top-ranked West Virginia. Rising stars included Kansas's Wilt Chamberlain, Cincinnati's Oscar Robertson, and Elgin Baylor, Seattle.

## BOXING

**Sugar Ray Robinson**, 37, regained his middleweight title, but he had to go the 15-round distance to do so. Heavyweight **Floyd Patterson** put Texan Roy Harris away in the 12th round. An aging **Archie Moore** successfully defended his light heavyweight title against Canadian opponent Yvon Durelle, 29.

The **Milwaukee Braves** and the **New York Yankees** dominated season play. The Yankees were New York's only remaining major-league club, as the Dodgers and Giants had just finished their first season in their new western locations. The Yanks managed to win the Series—the hard way; it was their 18th title in the past 38 years, 8th in the past 12. Names to remember from the series were Hank Bauer, Whitey Ford, Bob Turley, and Don Larsen for the Yankees. Star catcher for the (now LA) Dodgers Roy Campanella was paralyzed from the neck down, as a result of a January auto accident. Stan Musial of the Cardinals scored his 3,000th major-league hit.

In collegiate play, Louisiana State University finished the season with a perfect record—unbeaten, untied. Pete Dawkins was awarded the Heisman trophy. In the NFL's most famous championship game, Johnny Unitas and the Baltimore Colts won their first championship, beating the New York Giants in sudden-death overtime, the first ever played in an official league game. Jim Brown was in his second pro year, with the Cleveland Browns.

# sports

**Edson Arantes do Nascimento of Brazil became known simply as Pele, King of Soccer, after leading Brazil to World Cup success over Sweden.**

BOBBY FISCHER, OF BROOKLYN, BECAME U.S. CHESS CHAMPION AT 15.

*Gigi* scored big on Oscar night (April 6, 1959); it took Best Picture honors, Best Directing award for Vincente Minnelli, writing honors for Alan Jay Lerner, awards for art direction and film editing, Best Song for "Gigi," the title tune, and best scoring of a musical picture. **Susan Hayward** was named Best Actress for her role as a prostitute who goes to the gas chamber in spite of doubts about her guilt in *I Want To Live!*. The other nominees were Deborah Kerr, for *Separate Tables,* Shirley MacLaine in *Some Came Running,* Rosalind Russell's *Auntie Mame,* and Elizabeth Taylor in *Cat On a Hot Tin Roof.* **David Niven** won Best Actor Oscar for *Separate Tables.*

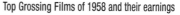

Top Grossing Films of 1958 and their earnings
1. **The Bridge on the River Kwai** $18,000,000
2. **Peyton Place** $12,000,000
3. **Sayonara** $10,500,000
4. **No Time for Sergeants** $7,200,000
5. **The Vikings** $7,000,000
6. **Search for Paradise** $6,500,000
7. **South Pacific** $6,400,000
8. **Cat on a Hot Tin Roof** $6,100,000
9. **Raintree County** $6,000,000
10. **Old Yeller** $5,900,000

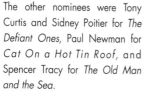

The other nominees were Tony Curtis and Sidney Poitier for *The Defiant Ones,* Paul Newman for *Cat On a Hot Tin Roof,* and Spencer Tracy for *The Old Man and the Sea.*

**Burl Ives** *(The Big Country)* was named Best Supporting Actor. **Wendy Hiller** *(Separate Tables)* got the Supporting Actress Oscar. The French film **My Uncle** was named Best Foreign Language Film.

# cars

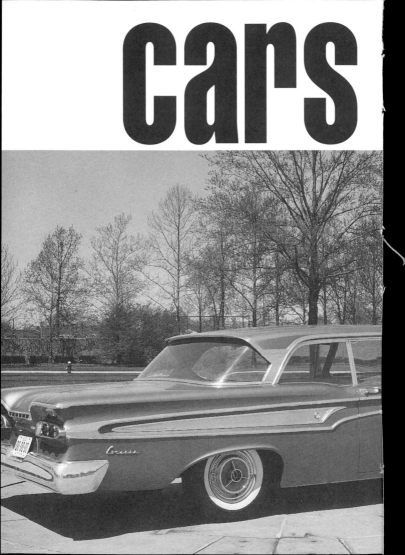

## THE STATION WAGON CONTINUED IN GAINING MARKET SHARE, REACHING ALMOST 15 PERCENT.

**The Edsel**, introduced in September 1957, developed into a full-fledged debacle and automotive laughingstock. The poet Marianne Moore had been hired to conceive a name for it, but her suggestions were rejected, and the car was named after Henry Ford's father. The Edsel's most distinctive feature was its vertical grille; some said it looked like an Oldsmobile sucking a lemon, and others saw more resemblance to female genitalia. So many Edsels were given away in contests that almost every Edsel owner found himself being asked, "Where did you win yours?"

21

both unmistakably *brood,* world's finest natural gunmetal mutation mink...

LUTETIA RITTER ORIGINALS, New York

...f beauties, a wide-swinging stole, newly rounded at the ends, and a straight little jacket, both in the shadowed magnificence of "Lutetia"*
natural gunmetal mutation mink.   RITTER BROS., NEW YORK AND MONTREAL  •  H. P. WASSON, INDIANAPOLIS  •  FOLEY BROS., HOUSTON, TEXAS

*Mutation Mink Breeders Association     Virginia Thoren     Jewels—CARTIER     Hats—Mr. John

**The chemise**, or sack dress, was here to stay, but with endless variations on the basic shape. St. Laurent, Dior's successor, offered the Trapeze, Cardin the Sickle shape, Jacques Heim the Egg-Cup Silhouette. Other designers produced the "flounce," the side-draped "toga coat," and the "sling drape." The basic oval shape all these were based on was inspired by the shape of space rockets. Skirts were getting shorter, outlines looser—touching the body only at the hipline. One flattering variation was the high-waisted Empire or Directoire. Audrey Hepburn, who was one of the 12 "best-dressed" women, carried this look off smashingly.

FLUFFY, PETALLIKE, OR FEATHERY EFFECTS APPEARED IN HAIR AND HATS. THE "TOSSED SALAD" LOOK WAS PERHAPS THE MOST POPULAR "DO."

**Furs** had a great resurgence. The industry promoted touches of mink on the oddest things: three mink-trimmed golf tees for $1, mink-trimmed coasters, even a furry telephone slipcover. Fur trim appeared at hemlines and on housecoats. A sable greatcoat cost $65,000. For the more discreet, a sable-lined raincoat could be had for $15,000.

# fashion

**In menswear**, paisley continued to be popular in ties, jacket linings, handkerchiefs, and scarves. Suit trousers were more tapered, often cuffless, and jackets were narrower and slimmer. Shawl collars were fashionable on men's jackets. The Italian influence was evident in shoes, with suede and soft leathers used in pointier-toed styles. Bulky knit sportswear was big. Short-sleeved sweaters in cashmere, wool, or cotton knit were increasingly popular.

# final factoid

**"Parenting"** was the brand-new term for supervising your children. **"Overkill"** was new, as were **"summitry," "hot dog"** as applied to a race driver, and **"psychic energizer,"** a drug to increase mental activity. Also first noted in 1958 were **"sex kitten,"** for a sexy, cuddly actress, and the **"sick joke."**

## credits

archive photos: inside front cover, pages 1, 6, 15, 20, 24, inside back cover.

associated press: pages 2, 5, 10.

photofest: pages 7, 8, 9, 10, 13, 16, 18.

original photography:
beth phillips: pages 13.

photo research:
alice albert

coordination:
rustyn birch

design:
carol bokuniewicz design
paul ritter